FROGS AND TOADS

Text: Maria Àngels Julivert
Illustrations: Marcel Socías Studios

Consulting Editor: Fredric L. Frye, DVM. MS, Fellow
Royal Society of Medicine

English translation © 1993 by Barron's Educational Series, Inc.

© Parramón Ediciones, S.A. 1993.

The title of the Spanish edition is *El fascinante mundo de
las ranas y las sapos.*

Published by Parramón Ediciones. S.A., Barcelona, Spain

All inquiries should be addressed to:
Barron's Educational Series, Inc.
250 Wireless Boulevard
Hauppauge, New York 11788

International Standard Book No. 0-8120-1565-7 (paperback)
International Standard Book No. 0-8120-6345-7 (hardcover)

Library of Congress Catalog Card No. 92-45635

Library of Congress Cataloging-in-Publication Data
Julivert, Angels.
    [Fascinante mundo de las ranas y las sapos. English]
    The fascinating world of frogs and toads / [text, Maria Angels
Julivert ; illustrations, Marcel Socías Studios].
        p.   cm.
    Includes index.
    Summary: Describes the physical characterisics, behavior, and
habitats of various kinds of frogs and toads.
    ISBN 0-8120-1565-7
    1. Frogs—Juvenile literature.   2. Toads—Juvenile literature.
[1. Frogs.   2. Toads.]   I. Title.
QL668.E2J8513   1993
597.8—dc20   92-45635
                                         CIP
                                         AC

Printed in Spain
3456   9960   98765432

THE FASCINATING WORLD OF

FROGS AND TOADS

FOREST HOUSE ®

School & Library Edition

A DOUBLE LIFE

Amphibians were the first **vertebrates** (animals with a backbone) to leave the water and start living on land. They did this some three hundred million years ago. To this class of animals belong the frogs, toads, salamanders, and newts.

Frogs and toads belong to the order of **Anura**. They can be identified by a chubby body and bulging eyes.

In some species, eardrums are easily distinguishable behind the eyes.

Most frogs and toads, like other amphibians, spend part of their life in the water and part out of it.

During the first stages of their life, they are **aquatic**. They breathe through **gills**, and have a long tail. Later, most adults can live on land. They have lost their tails and breathe through lungs. They also can exchange oxygen and carbon dioxide through the skin.

The rear legs of anurans are much longer than the front ones. This makes them excellent jumpers.

The skin of frogs and toads, which they shed from time to time, has no hairs, scales, or feathers to protect it. Frogs have a large number of mucus-secreting glands that keep the skin wet. Some species also have glands that secrete highly poisonous substances.

Right: Frogs and toads are amphibians—animals that spend much of their life in the water and only a part of it on land. When they are adults, they breathe through their lungs. Having lungs enables them to hunt on land ①. When they are at home in the water, they must come up to the surface to breathe in air ② and ③.

PUPIL SHAPES

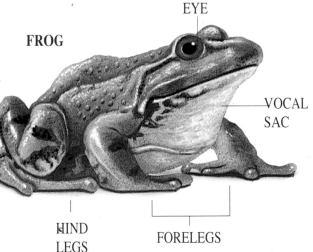

FROG

EYE

VOCAL SAC

HIND LEGS

FORELEGS

HEART

VERTICAL

TOAD

Top and left: There are countless species of frogs and toads. The different varieties are distinguished by the size of their legs and the texture and color of their skin.

HORIZONTAL

ROUND

THE FROGS

Among the more than 2,000 species of anurans, there are frogs and toads that differ widely in appearance, size, and habits.

Frogs have smooth, wet skin and make large jumps with their long rear legs. Most of them are great swimmers. They live near lakes, marshes, streams, and streamlets.

To this family belong some of the best-known anurans. Most of them are medium size, but some species are impressively large. The bullfrog of North America and the Goliath frog of Africa are the largest ones. The Goliath frog can reach more than 8 inches (20 cm.) in length. Frogs of this family are divided into two groups: green and brown. The green frogs spend much time in the water. They have large round eyes and the males possess two vocal sacs that bulge when they croak. Some of them

have a loud voice, and when they sing in "chorus" they can be very noisy.

Most brown frogs are not as aquatic as green ones. Some of them live far from water—except during mating season. They have more widely separated eyes and the vocal sacs of males are deep inside the body.

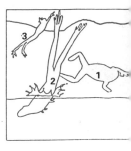

Right: The pond is the frog's main **habitat**. Here you can see frogs swimming ①, diving ②, and doing spectacular leaps ③.

Below: There is a great variety of frogs—green frogs, brown frogs, and even some that look like toads.

GREEN FROG

RED FROG

Below: The green areas of the map show where frogs are found.

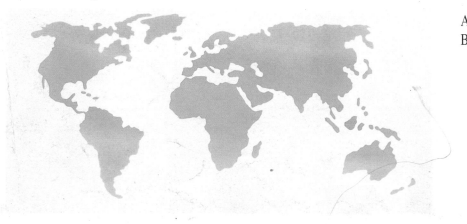

AFRICAN BULL FROG

THE TOADS

Toads have a chubby body and dry skin that is full of warts. They can be found all over the world, except in frigid polar regions.

Many toads are chubbier than frogs and some of them live far from water. They quite often walk rather than jump, because their legs are shorter than frogs' legs.

Toads have a pair of glands behind the eyes that produce toxic secretions. Although not usually dangerous to humans, they can cause irritation to sensitive tissues, such as the eyes. In some species, these glands, called **parotids**, are enormous.

The common toad has very bumpy skin and large parotid glands. During the day it stays hidden in a cool shelter.

In the evening, it leaves its refuge to look for insects, worms, and other **invertebrates** to feed on. It captures its prey with its tongue, which can reach far out like that of frogs.

Year after year, the common toad returns to the same watery places to reproduce.

The female, much larger than the male, lays long strings of eggs in the water. The small polywogs or tadpoles are black and take several months to become little toads.

The marine toad belongs to the same family. It can be more than 8 inches (20 cm.) long and it is one of the largest anurans. Its skin secretions are quite poisonous.

Top: Like this marine toad, most toads are covered with warts. They also have glands that produce a poisonous fluid.

Right: In the small illustrations you can see the glands of a common toad and those of a green toad.

Right: Toads spend less time in the water than frogs. You will find them most often on land ①. Many of them spend the day hidden under rocks ② or in their nests ③ and only come out at night.

POISONOUS GLANDS

SLANTED

Left: The green areas of the map show where toads live. The different types of toads live in different habitats—such as gardens, fields, forests, and jungles.

PARALLEL

THE SINGING MALES

Most anurans reproduce once a year, usually in the spring, when food is plentiful and the weather is milder. In this season, hundreds of frogs and toads may gather by lakes, rivers, springs, and pools. The moment to look for a partner has arrived.

Males are the first to reach the water. With their croaking, they attempt to attract females toward the places chosen for courtship, mating, and laying eggs. Sometimes these sounds are heard for long distances.

Every frog and toad has a characteristic call. This way the females can recognize the males of their species.

The males of some species possess **vocal sacs**, which expand when singing. They can have a pair of them, such as those of the common green frog. These vocal sacs are located in the corners of the mouth.

Many others just have one vocal sac, which is situated below the throat, like that found in many toads.

The vocal sacs of many anurans are external and expand extraordinarily when the frog or toad is croaking. Many other males possess internal vocal sacs that are scarcely seen.

During the breeding season, males of some species develop warty pads on their legs to help hold the slippery females.

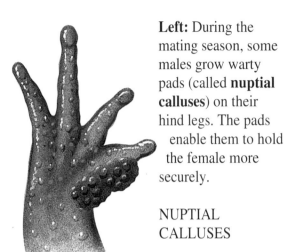

Left: During the mating season, some males grow warty pads (called **nuptial calluses**) on their hind legs. The pads enable them to hold the female more securely.

NUPTIAL CALLUSES

Right: During the mating season, the males of certain species fight each other. These battles are rituals. The contestants don't actually hurt each other.

Right: At certain times of the year, frogs and toads go to lakes and ponds to mate. The male attracts the female ① with his noisy call. Some male frogs have only one vocal sac ②; others possess two ③; and some frogs have internal vocal sacs, which are hardly noticeable.

BATTLE BETWEEN MALES

LAYING THE EGGS

Most of the frogs and toads mate in the water. Only a few species reproduce on land. Others breed in trees, depositing their eggs in pools of water trapped in leaves and flowers.

During the mating, the male embraces the female with the front legs, holding her firmly. The female lays many eggs that the male fertilizes with his sperm. The eggs are small and round and have a protective jelly-like coating.

Eggs can be laid in small packs, long strings, or large groups.

Usually they are abandoned in the water and are not cared for any longer. These eggs are left either fastened to aquatic plants or floating freely. Others are attended to by the female from time to time.

Some frogs protect their eggs in foam nests that they prepare. These little frogs secrete a jellied substance that they whip up with their rear legs until enough foam is formed. They lay their eggs inside this foam.

The outer part of this strange nest gets dry in contact with the air, but inside it is wet.

Some days later, the tadpoles mature and they fall into the water as the nest breaks apart.

Other frogs dam up a small body of water with mud. Inside this temporary pond they lay the eggs.

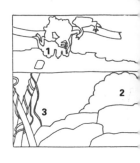

Right: The females lay their eggs in different ways: in foam nests ①, in clumps ②, and in chains ③.

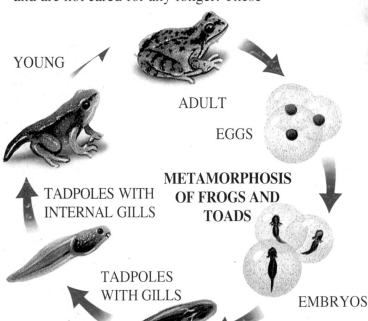

YOUNG

ADULT

EGGS

METAMORPHOSIS OF FROGS AND TOADS

TADPOLES WITH INTERNAL GILLS

TADPOLES WITH GILLS

EMBRYOS

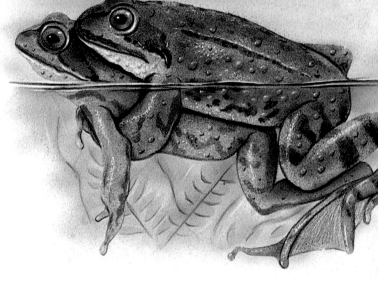

Top: When mating, the male mounts the female and hugs her tightly. This usually takes place in the water. While the female lays the eggs the male fertilizes them.

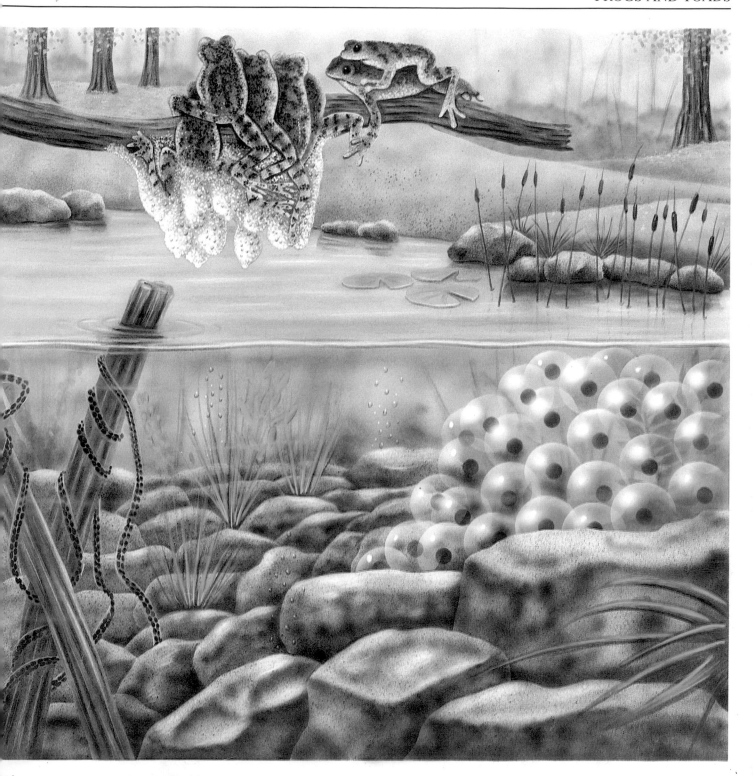

THE PARENTS' CARE

Some species of frogs and toads devote special care to their eggs and larvae. The males of the nurse toad, for instance, carry the eggs until the tadpoles are born.

During the mating, that takes place on land, the male wraps the string of fertilized eggs around his rear legs. During the day he remains hidden under stones or in some hole and only emerges at night.

From time to time, he approaches the water to moisten the eggs. Finally, during one of these visits to the water, the tadpoles leave their eggs and fall into the water where they remain until they grow into little toads.

The females of other species, such as the marsupial frog from South America, have a pouch on the back where they put the eggs once they are fertilized. When the larvae are born, the mother opens the pouch with her legs and sets the tadpoles free in the water.

The behavior of the Darwin frog is quite amusing. The females of this species lay their eggs on the ground. The males (that are nearby watching the process) swallow the fertilized eggs and keep them inside a kind of sack in the throat.

The tadpoles remain in this safe shelter within their father until their development ends.

Right: The nurse toad collects the eggs between its hind legs ① and wets them ②. When the eggs hatch the tadpoles fall into the water ③.

MARSUPIAL FROG

DARWIN FROG

Left: The marsupial frog carries its eggs in a pouch on its back.

Top: The Darwin frog lays its eggs on the ground. The male then takes them in h mouth and carries them in a special sac in which they develo

AN EXTRAORDI-NARY CHANGE

The young of frogs and toads emerge from the eggs as tiny fish-like creatures. These are the tadpoles. At the beginning they scarcely move and fasten themselves to aquatic plants by means of suckers. Some days later, they start swimming about.

The tadpoles do not resemble the adults at all. They have a long tail, lack legs, and breathe through gills.

Tadpoles are aquatic and experience an unbelievable transformation during which the body goes through major changes, both internal and external.This process is called **metamorphosis**.

The body changes gradually. Legs grow (the rear legs appear first, then the front ones). Little by little the tadpole's body gets longer and the tail gets shorter. Gills disappear and the lungs develop.

When the metamorphosis is complete, the tadpoles leave the water in the shape of little frogs and toads, eager to start life on land.

LAYING AND HATCHING OF EGGS

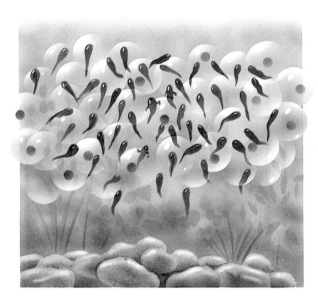

Right: Finally, the eggs hatch and the tadpoles emerge ①. Little by little they are transformed. Firs they develop hind ar front legs ② and ③ their tail becomes shorter ④. Later, the tail disappears and young frogs can leav the water. The metamorphosis is now complete ⑤.

A POND CON-STRUCTED BY AI ARTIFICER FROG

Left: The artificer frog is one of the fev species that con-structs a kind of shelter to protect the embryos and newly born tadpoles. This construction is a small pond, made near the shore with walls of mud.

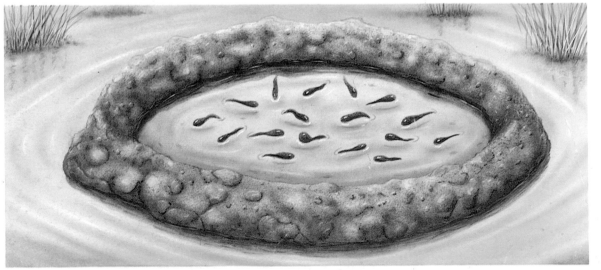

A VERY STICKY TONGUE

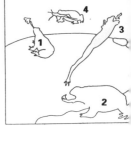

Adult frogs and toads are **carnivorous**, which means they feed on other animals. They capture spiders and worms, as well as fish, mollusks, and other frogs. They are also great devourers of insects, many of them harmful to agriculture. That is why frogs and toads are advantageous for humans and we should feel friendly toward them.

The tadpoles' diet is different: they mainly feed on algae, though they also eat plants and decomposing animals.

The tongue of frogs and toads is covered with a slimy mucus to which the prey

HORNED FROG

Below: Some species of frogs and toads can swallow whole rodents.

Top: Tadpoles feed on water plants.

Right: Frogs and toads have different hunting methods. They can reach out their tongues for considerable distances ① and trap insects ②, or perform extraordinary leaps to catch their prey ③. They can also hunt on land ④.

adheres. In some species the tongue is also **protractile**. This means they can extend it far out of the mouth.

Many frogs can catch flying insects by means of a great and accurate jump.

Frogs and toads usually hunt in ambush and remain still for hours waiting for some little animal. Larger anurans even can capture lizards and other small vertebrates.

The horned frog often hunts little mice that it catches and bites with its strong jaws. This amphibian with a chubby body and short legs is quite aggressive. It lives in the wet South American forests and hides very well amid plentiful vegetation.

ESCAPE AND CAMOUFLAGE

Frogs and toads have many enemies: snakes, birds of prey, and mammals are some of them. Several birds, such as herons and cranes, also capture tadpoles and many fish love these amphibians and their eggs.

To avoid being eaten, frogs and toads resort to all kinds of tricks. Most of them escape in large jumps or plunge into the water looking for a place to hide. Many species **camouflage** themselves very well in their surroundings due to the color and pattern of their skin. The leaf frog stays undetected, hidden among the fallen leaves. The shape and color of its body is almost identical to those of a leaf.

When escape is not possible, some species adopt threatening attitudes. The common toad swells up, lowers its head, and stretches its rear legs to appear larger in front of an enemy.

Others have showy colors and patterns that they exhibit when they are in danger. The yellow belly toad turns its rear legs over and displays showy orangy-yellow color with blue spots, thus frightening its aproaching aggressor.

HORNED FROG

DARWIN FROG

STONE TOAD

Right: Frogs and toads have many enemies, including birds, mammals ①, snakes that can swallow them whole ②, and also salamanders (which eat their eggs) ③. To avoid being eaten, frogs either escape, camouflage themselves, or try to mak themselves appear bigger than they really are by blowin up their bodies ④.

Left and top: Thes two frogs camoufla themselves by mimicking the colo and shape of leaves

Left: This toad hide under stones or leav during the day, blending in with th background.

A VERY PECULIAR FAMILY

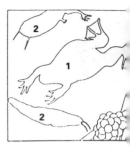

Some frogs spend their whole lives in the water, such as the pipa and the clawed frog. Both of them are great swimmers. They have membranes between their toes to help them swim faster. These two species, which belong to the same family, are among the few anurans that lack a protractile tongue.

The pipa is a curious frog with a flat body and tiny eyes. It lives in the rivers and streams of certain South American regions.

During mating, the pipas turn around and around. The eggs are laid on the female's back and are covered by a thin layer of skin. Each egg rests inside a small, individual cavity.

The tadpoles develop inside these little cavities and emerge as froglets.

The clawed frog, also aquatic, comes from Africa. It received its name because it has three nails on the toes of the rear legs. It has a wide mouth and feeds on crustaceans, insects, small fish, and so on.

MATING DANCE OF THE PIPA FROG

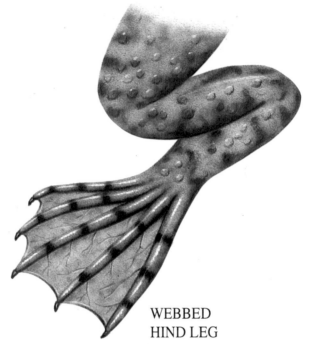

WEBBED
HIND LEG

When the marshes, pools, and streams where it lives dry up, the clawed frog buries itself in the mud until the first rains arrive. Reproduction takes place during the rainy season. The female lays small eggs that stick to aquatic plants.

The larvae of this species are quite different from the ordinary tadpole. They have two long whiskers on the snout and look like catfish.

Right: The clawed frog ① spends its entire life in the water. The young ② do not look very much like other tadpoles.

Below: The pipa fro is another totally aquatic frog. When pair mate, they perform a curious dance. The male collects the eggs and deposits them on the female's back.

SMALL BUT DANGEROUS

S ome frogs do not need to hide or remain undetected because they are poisonous. On the contrary, their showy colors are a warning to the other animals.

These frogs have poison glands scattered all over their body.

The effect of their poison depends on the size of the animal that it affects. It is mainly dangerous to small animals.

In South American rainforests, some frogs live that measure only 1¼ to 1½ inches (3–4 cm.) long. In spite of being so small, they are very dangerous. There are several species and all of them have showy colors: some of them are red with bluish legs, some others are yellow or green with black spots.

The Indians of the forest rub the poisonous secretions from these frogs on the darts

POISON ARROW FROG

STRAWBERRY FROG

Right: Poisonous frogs are often identifiable by their brightly colored markings. This is an effective defense system. There are many such specie of varying color

Left: In the tropical forests of South America live the Dendrobate species of frogs. Yo can see some in the pictures on this page They are very small: between ¾ of an inc and 1½ inches (2–4 cm) in length. Their poison, however, is very strong and can kill a small animal.

with which they hunt birds, monkeys, and squirrels. The poison, which is quite potent, is absorbed into the animal's blood, paralyzing or killing the victim. In order to obtain the poison, the Indians heat the little frogs in a fire and collect the poison as it oozes out of the frogs' skin.

MANTELED FROG

LIVING UNDER THE SOIL

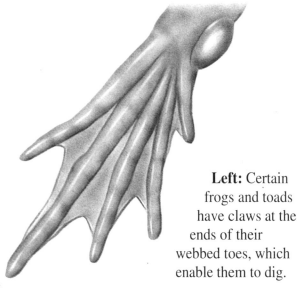

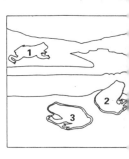

There are anurans that prefer living underground, because they feel safer there. There are also species that hide under stones, among the rocks, or in some animal's cave during the day.

Many toads and frogs bury themselves during certain periods of the year. The remainder of life is spent out in the open air.

In cold climates, anurans spend winter in holes or burrows, or buried in the mud of pools or ponds. They do not leave their shelter until spring has arrived.

The species that live in warm climates spend the hotter and drier season resting. In Australian deserts, there are frogs that stay buried in the sand for several months. When the rains arrive, the frogs leave their refuge to reproduce. Because they breathe through their skin, they can stay buried a long time without coming to the surface.

Left: Certain frogs and toads have claws at the ends of their webbed toes, which enable them to dig.

A few anurans can dig their own burrows. They are fully adapted to underground life and possess special structures with which to dig. They excavate holes where they spend most of their time. They only emerge to hunt and reproduce.

The spur toad has a horny spur, hard and sharp, in the rear legs, which it uses to dig tunnels in soft, sandy areas.

Right: Frogs and toads are cold-blooded. Unlike bird and mammals, they cannot produce heat to regulate their bodily temperature. For this reason, they search for a warm place in winter—normally by digging into the bank ① or the bottom of a pond ②. Other species bury themselves completely ③.

Below: The spade-footed toad uses its hind feet to burrow into the earth.

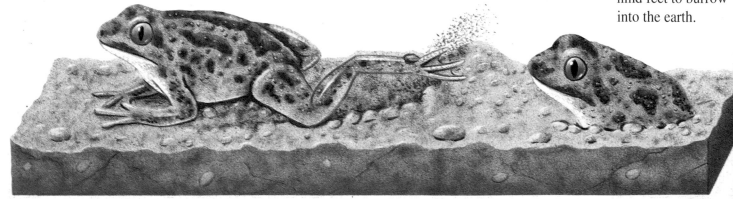

LIFE IN THE TREES

Some anurans spend their whole lives in the water. Others prefer to live on land or in trees.

Tree frogs have adhesive suckers on the tip of their toes with which they can fasten themselves, even to a glass surface. They are very quick and climb easily in trees and bushes. Only rarely do they come down to the ground.

In Europe, there are two very well-known tree frogs: St. Anthony's frog and the southern frog. They are very much alike because of both their appearance and their behavior. They scarcely measure 2 inches (5 cm.) long and have varied colors. Most of them are green, but there are also yellowish, brown, and even blue frogs.

St. Anthony's frog has a dark stripe along its side. The southern frog has a much shorter stripe that reaches just its front legs. They hunt at night and usually remain still during the day. With their legs close to the

FOOT OF A TREE FROG

SUCTION CUP

Right: Some frogs spend their lives attached to trees and bushes, coming down only to reproduce.

Left: Tree frogs have something similar to suction cups on their toes. This allows them to stick to all kinds of surfaces, however smooth they may be.

TREE FROG

body, they are well hidden among the vegetation. In the spring both types go down to ponds and pools to reproduce.

Some kinds of tree frogs never come down to the ground. They even mate and lay the eggs among the trees and bushes. The flying frogs build foam nests that they place on the leaves and branches hanging over the water. Do you remember how they prepare these nests?

Glossary

amphibian. A type of vertebrate animal that develops from a legless tadpole. Tadpoles are aquatic and breathe through gills. However, many adult amphibians, which breathe through lungs, can live on land.

anuran. An order of amphibians that do not have tails. Frogs and toads are anurans.

aquatic. Plants or animals that live in the water.

camouflage. Colors and patterns that enable a creature to blend with its background.

carnivorous. Animals that feed on other animals.

gills. The breathing organ of aquatic animals, such as the amphibian tadpoles and fish.

habitat. The place where a plant or animal lives.

invertebrates. Animals that lack a backbone. Insects, worms, and snails are invertebrates.

metamorphosis. The total transformation of the body of a tadpole during its development. The phases are: egg, embryo, tadpole, and adult frog or toad.

nuptial calluses. Warty pads that enable some male anurans to grasp the female during mating.

parotid glands. Glands situated behind the eyes whose secretion is toxic. These glands are common in certain anurans.

protractile. Able to be thrust out; in this case, a tongue that can reach far out of the mouth.

vertebrates. Animals that possess a backbone and an internal skeleton. Fish, mammals, birds, reptiles, and amphibians are vertebrates.

vocal sac. Skin bags that most male anurans possess to amplify the sound of their song or croak.

ndex